Original title:
Cozy Nooks and Frosty Windows

Copyright © 2024 Creative Arts Management OÜ
All rights reserved.

Author: Milo Harrington
ISBN HARDBACK: 978-9916-94-438-7
ISBN PAPERBACK: 978-9916-94-439-4

Sipping Serenity in Winter Light

A cup of warmth in chilly air,
Snowflakes dance without a care,
The gentle glow of twilight's grace,
A moment found, a quiet space.

Fires crackle, shadows play,
Whispers of the end of day,
Outside, the world is soft and white,
Inside, hearts bask in cozy light.

Evening's Glow Behind Crystal Walls

The sun dips low, a golden hue,
Crystal panes reflect the view,
Colors blend in soft embrace,
Painting stillness on each face.

Laughter echoes, stories flow,
In this warmth, the chill won't grow,
Outside, winter keeps its hold,
Inside, memories turn to gold.

Cozy Embrace without the Name

Blankets piled, a fortress made,
Time stands still, and worries fade,
In the softness, hearts connect,
Unspoken love that we protect.

Silent moments, tender sighs,
Only warmth, no goodbyes,
Every heartbeat shares the flame,
In this hush, we know no name.

Comfort's Warmth on a Chilling Night

Stars above, a twinkling sight,
Wrapped in peace, the world feels right,
A gentle breeze, a night so still,
With every breath, our hearts can fill.

Fires glow, shadows play,
Binding us in night's ballet,
Every moment feels so bright,
In comfort's warmth on this chill night.

Whispers in the Snug

In the corner, shadows play,
Warm light flickers, night holds sway.
Gentle murmurs, secrets told,
Softly wrapped in comfort bold.

A crackling fire, embers glow,
Whispers dance, while outside snow.
Cobweb dreams, our hearts entwined,
In this snug, our peace we find.

The Gentle Embrace of Winter's Heart

Snowflakes fall like whispered sighs,
Blanketing the world, soft and wise.
Crisp air brings a tranquil grace,
Nature pauses, slows its pace.

Frosted trees in silence stand,
Winter paints with a gentle hand.
A hush descends, serene and bright,
As day surrenders into night.

Solitary Reflections by Candlelight

Candle flickers, shadows loom,
Thoughts drift softly, fill the room.
Memories whispered, voices near,
In solitude, I find my cheer.

Flickering flame, a quiet guide,
Where dreams and wishes gently bide.
In each glow, a story's thread,
In the silence, truths are spread.

The Hidden Bower's Warmth

Nestled deep where secrets grow,
In the bower, soft winds blow.
Nature's cradle, soft and sweet,
A hidden warmth beneath our feet.

Sunlight dapples, leaves do sway,
In this haven, time slips away.
With every breath, the world does fade,
In the whispering shade, hope is laid.

The Shelter of Silence

In the quiet, shadows blend,
Whispers dance, no need to mend.
Night wraps softly, dreams take flight,
In the hush, we find our light.

Stars above begin to hum,
In stillness, heartbeats drum.
Sheltered by the calm embrace,
Time stands still, a sacred space.

Voices fade, thoughts intertwine,
Lost in moments, yours and mine.
In the silence, bonds are drawn,
A gentle peace greets the dawn.

Melodies of the Flickering Fire

Crackling embers sing a tune,
As shadows dance beneath the moon.
Each flicker tells a tale of old,
Of warmth and love in the night so bold.

Around the flame, we gather near,
With laughter, joy, and stories dear.
The melody swells, hearts entwine,
In the glow, a spirit divine.

Sparks like wishes rise and gleam,
We share our hopes, ignite the dream.
As night wanes, the fire sighs,
Its soft embrace, where comfort lies.

On the Edge of Warmth

The sun dips low, a golden hue,
Inviting stars to pierce the blue.
With every breath, the evening sighs,
As shadows stretch and daylight dies.

In the edges of twilight's grace,
We find our peace, a soft embrace.
The world urges us to retreat,
But here together, life is sweet.

With laughter shared and stories spun,
Moments linger, never done.
On this brink, where hearts align,
We hold the day's last spark divine.

The Glow of Togetherness

In the circle, warmth draws near,
Shared smiles and laughter fill the sphere.
Hands entwined in silent grace,
In this glow, we find our place.

Every heartbeat, a soothing sound,
In every glance, love is found.
As we celebrate the simple ties,
Togetherness lights up the skies.

Memories made, etched in time,
In this haven, all feels prime.
With every moment, joy reveals,
The power of love and how it heals.

The Quiet of a Winter Evening

Snowflakes fall like whispers,
Covering the world in peace.
The moon hangs low and silver,
As time seems to gently cease.

The cold air bites and dances,
While shadows stretch and play.
In this calm, a stillness glances,
At the end of a fading day.

Fires crackle softly, glowing,
Warmth wrapped in quiet sighs.
Outside, the wind is blowing,
But inside, comfort lies.

In the hush of night's embrace,
Thoughts drift like snow in flight.
Winter's grace, a soft trace,
In the beauty of the night.

Rooms Filled with Laughter and Light

Laughter dances on the walls,
Bouncing off with each sweet sound.
Joy erupts in joyful calls,
As love and warmth surround.

Sunlight spills through open blinds,
Painting smiles across the space.
In every heart, a treasure finds,
Its place in this embrace.

Friends gather near, stories flow,
Moments cherished, spirits bright.
In this haven, joy will grow,
Filling rooms with pure delight.

Time stands still, but love ignites,
Memories woven in the night.
In these rooms filled with laughter,
We find our joy, our ever after.

A Safe Haven in the Chill

In the corners of my mind, a flame,
Whispers of warmth, calling my name.
Through the frost that nips at my skin,
I find solace where love begins.

Blankets wrapped like a tender embrace,
In this sanctuary, I find my place.
The world outside is a wintry plight,
Yet here, the heart dances in light.

Fireflies of Warmth in the Air

Dancing softly, flickering bright,
Fireflies weave in the cool night.
They bring stories of summer's grace,
As the chill fades with each embrace.

Their glow wraps around like a friend,
In fleeting moments that just won't end.
These tiny lanterns spark delight,
Guiding hearts towards the light.

Hiding from the White Outside

Outside the world wears a coat of snow,
But in this nook, my warmth does grow.
Walls of timber, a refuge secured,
Here in the quiet, my soul is assured.

I watch as winter dances and twirls,
While here I sip on dreams unfurls.
In this safe space, the heart can roam,
As the white outside whispers, 'Welcome home.'

The Serendipity of Stillness

In the hush of evening's gentle sigh,
Moments linger like stars in the sky.
Each breath a treasure, a rare delight,
In stillness, the heart takes flight.

When time stands still, the spirit is free,
Finding beauty in simplicity.
In quietude, the world slows down,
A crown of peace, my cherished crown.

Winter's Gentle Drift

Snowflakes dance in twilight's gleam,
Blankets soft on every seam.
Whispers flow from branches bare,
Nature's hush is everywhere.

Footprints trace a fleeting path,
Time slows down, a gentle math.
Fires crackle with warmth and light,
Winter's magic, pure delight.

Cold winds sing a lullaby,
Stars peer down from velvet sky.
Silent nights enfold the earth,
In winter's arms, we find rebirth.

Whispers Beneath the Eiderdown

Softly, dreams begin to stir,
Wrapped in warmth, emotions purr.
Firelight flickers on the wall,
As winter's shadows rise and fall.

Underneath the quilted dreams,
Laughter floats like gentle beams.
Stories shared in cozy light,
Whispers weave through tranquil night.

Silken threads of night unfold,
As tales emerge, both new and old.
Time stands still, a precious find,
In eiderdown, our hearts aligned.

Pale Light Through Snowy Sashes

Morning breaks, a soft embrace,
Pale light spills on nature's face.
Through the windows, frosted glass,
World transformed as moments pass.

Icicles hang like crystal tears,
Echoes of forgotten years.
Each breath puffs like tender smoke,
In winter's grip, we laugh and soak.

Rays of sun on silver snow,
Nature's spark begins to glow.
Quiet beauty, pure and bright,
Whispers linger, day and night.

Snowbound Secrets

Hidden paths through drifts of white,
Secrets murmur in the night.
Frosted trees, a silent choir,
Guarding dreams, we dare not tire.

Underneath the blankets deep,
Winter's treasures gently sleep.
Stories buried, lost in time,
Await the heart to bring to rhyme.

Games are played with shadowed hints,
Snowbound secrets, nature prints.
As the seasons softly change,
Whispers shift, both sweet and strange.

Serene Spaces Wrapped in Wool

In the corners, shadows blend,
Softly whisper, time to mend.
Warmth embraces, quiet sighs,
As the world outside it lies.

Blankets piled, a gentle view,
Colors soft in every hue.
Tucked in close, the cold retreats,
Here in wool, the heart it beats.

Moments linger, stillness grow,
Wrapped in layers, soft and slow.
Serenity in every fold,
In these spaces, dreams unfold.

Firelight Reflections on Panes

Dancing flames, a flicker's glow,
Casting warmth on the falling snow.
Glass adorned with shimmering light,
Whispers of an enchanting night.

Crackling wood, the soothing sound,
Within these walls, peace is found.
Reflections waltz upon the glass,
Moments cherished, wishing they last.

Glimmers trace the patterns made,
In this haven, fears do fade.
Firelight's glow, a tender embrace,
Within its warmth, we find our place.

A Nest of Quietude

Stolen hours in a cozy nook,
Pages turned, the world they took.
Nestled deep in pillows' grace,
In this peace, we find our space.

Gentle whispers, stories told,
Moments bask in quiet gold.
Time stands still in this retreat,
A serene heartbeat, soft and sweet.

Outside storms may howl and rage,
Yet here we turn another page.
Wrapped in comfort's soft cocoon,
In this nest, we find our tune.

Comfort in the Heart of Winter

Snowflakes dancing, a silent fall,
Nature's blanket, covering all.
Inside, the hearth's warm embrace,
In winter's grip, we find our grace.

Mugs of cocoa, steam rising high,
Laughter mingling, spirits fly.
Fireside tales that warm the chill,
In the heart of winter, time stands still.

Days may shorten, darkness creep,
Yet in this warmth, dreams run deep.
Comfort cradled in every sigh,
In the heart of winter, we thrive.

Whispers of Warmth Beneath the Blanket

Under the quilt, we shuffle close,
Soft whispers blend with heartbeat's prose.
Fingers trace warmth on chilled skin,
Morning light dances, inviting us in.

The world outside, cold and stark,
While inside, our laughter ignites a spark.
Wrapped in dreams, we drift and sway,
In this cocoon, we choose to stay.

Frost-Kissed Glass and Fireside Dreams

Frosted windows, glimmering bright,
Tales of winter shared at night.
Dancing flames in the hearthlight glow,
We lose ourselves in stories slow.

The crackle speaks in whispered tones,
Comfort found in gentle moans.
With every sip, the warmth extends,
In our hearts, the chill rescends.

Embracing Hearthside Shadows

Shadows flicker, stories unfold,
Hearthside magic in the cold.
With every laugh, the warmth expands,
Comfort nestled in our hands.

The night wraps tight, a velvet cloak,
Around the fire, we softly stoke.
Embracing dreams till midnight breaks,
In these hours, our spirit wakes.

Winter Light through Softened Edges

Softened edges of the night,
Winter's breath, a gentle light.
Shadows linger, softly cast,
Moments cherished, shadows passed.

Through frosted panes, the world does gleam,
Reflecting warmth, a fleeting dream.
In the stillness, a heart aligns,
In winter's grip, our love defines.

Shadows Dancing in the Glow

In the twilight, shadows sway,
Casting dreams that drift away.
Whispers echo through the night,
Guided softly by the light.

Flickering flames, a subtle grace,
Painting patterns, a warm embrace.
Each movement tells a secret tale,
As night winds weave a gentle veil.

Echoes of Laughter by the Flames

Around the fire, spirits soar,
Echoes of laughter, tales of yore.
The crackling wood sings a tune,
Underneath the silver moon.

Faces glow in fiery light,
Moments cherished, pure delight.
With every story shared, we find,
The bonds of love, forever twined.

Finding Warmth Amongst the Chill

In the chill of winter's breath,
We seek warmth, defying death.
Hearts entwined beneath the frost,
In this cold, we find no loss.

Glimmers of hope light the way,
Through the shadows, come what may.
Together we endure the night,
Finding solace in the light.

Stitches of Love on a Frosty Night

Beneath the quilt, we stitch our dreams,
Warmth surrounds, or so it seems.
Threads of love weave tight and true,
In this silence, just me and you.

Snowflakes fall, a gentle grace,
Every flake holds a warm embrace.
Through the frost, our hearts will bloom,
Finding joy in winter's room.

Reflections on a Chilly Evening

In the stillness, whispers grow,
As twilight casts its gentle glow.
Shadows dance beneath the trees,
Brought to life by the evening breeze.

A pond mirrors the fading light,
Ripples touch as day turns night.
Each star begins its careful peek,
In the silence, the heart can speak.

Thoughts drift softly, like falling leaves,
Wrapped in warmth, the spirit believes.
Every moment savored sweet,
As the cold air wraps like a sheet.

Lost in contemplation's embrace,
Reflections linger, time can't erase.
A chill caresses, soothing and near,
In this evening, all feels clear.

Cuddle Against the Winter's Breath

Snowflakes scatter like whispered dreams,
A blanket of white, soft as it seems.
The world is hushed, wrapped up tight,
Cuddled close against winter's bite.

Firelight dances, shadows play,
Inviting warmth to chase chill away.
A mug of cocoa, rich and sweet,
Comfort awaits in this cozy retreat.

Outside, the chill wraps its icy hand,
But inside we're anchored, together we stand.
Blankets piled, laughter in the air,
Mirth flourishes in winter's snare.

Embracing the cold, we find delight,
In cuddles shared on this wintry night.
Together, we make our own kind of heat,
Against winter's breath, love feels complete.

Enclosed in Tranquil Dreams

Under the moon's soft, silvery hue,
A world of dreams begins anew.
Whispers of night cradle the soul,
Gentle echoes make the spirit whole.

Stars like jewels in velvet spread,
Guide us softly into our bed.
Thoughts drift slowly, a peaceful tide,
In tranquil dreams, we can safely confide.

A blanket of calm wraps around tight,
Each breath a sigh in the depth of night.
Thoughts alight on fanciful beams,
Enclosed in world of soothing dreams.

With every heartbeat, the silence speaks,
In the realm where solace seeks.
Hope dances softly in shadowed gleams,
As we float gently on tranquil dreams.

Glimmers of Light in Frosted Spaces

Morning breaks with a delicate sheen,
Frosted branches glimmer, a sight serene.
Sunlight kisses the icy ground,
As nature awakens with hushed sound.

A landscape dressed in diamonds bright,
Each crystal twinkles in pure delight.
Winter's breath adorns the air,
With magic woven everywhere.

Footprints crunch on the frosty lane,
Each step a whisper, joy in the pain.
In every corner, hope takes flight,
Glimmers of joy in frosted light.

As day unfolds, warmth starts to rise,
Dancing with shadows, they harmonize.
In the chill, we find our grace,
In glimmers of light in frosted spaces.

Spun from Shadows and Light

In the twilight's gentle sway,
Soft whispers dance and play.
The night unveils its art,
With dreams that softly start.

Parallel worlds entwine,
In silver strands that shine.
Where shadows cloak the day,
And light begins to sway.

Gentle Snowfall

Flakes descend like whispered sighs,
Blanketing the earth, it lies.
Each crystal, pure and bright,
Turns the world a soft white.

The silence holds the breath,
In winter's grasp, sweet death.
Yet life is there, concealed,
In the hearts that love revealed.

Warm Embrace

Underneath the cover's fold,
Find the warmth, the tales unfold.
With every touch and every glance,
Hearts awaken, start to dance.

In arms where comfort dwells,
The soul with love compels.
Moments linger, sweet and near,
In the warmth, we lose our fear.

An Invitation to the Warmth Within

Come and sit by the fire's glow,
Where stories of old begin to flow.
The world fades into night's embrace,
Find solace in this sacred space.

Let the flames ignite your dreams,
In flickering light, everything beams.
A journey inward, explore the grace,
In the warmth within, all fears erase.

Frosty Whispers and Fireside Tales

Whispers weave through chilly air,
As twilight settles, cold and fair.
Stories crackle like the flames,
Fireside warmth, heart's tender claims.

Frosty echoes paint the night,
Each word a soft, enchanting light.
Gather close, let spirits soar,
In each tale, we find us more.

Hushed Retreats in the Cold

In whispered breaths the night descends,
Soft blankets wrap like hidden friends.
The frost clings tight to hollow trees,
While silence stirs on winter's breeze.

Each flake that falls, a gentle sigh,
Underneath the vast, dark sky.
A warmth ignites from flickering fires,
As memories weave like fragile wires.

Lonely paths in moonlit glow,
Trace the steps where few dare go.
The world lies still, a frozen dream,
In hushed retreats, a secret seam.

Such tranquil hours, though cold outside,
Within these walls, our hearts confide.
A time to pause, reflect, renew,
In winter's grasp, our love rings true.

Glint of Candlelight on Ice

Candle flames dance, a soft embrace,
Casting gold upon the frozen space.
Each flicker tells of warmth within,
A gentle glow where love begins.

Outside the world is cold and gray,
But here, our hearts refuse to sway.
With every laugh, the shadows play,
Breaking the night, chasing fear away.

Through frosty panes, the starry gleam,
Reflects our hopes, ignites a dream.
In quiet moments, we find our grace,
As winter wraps us in its lace.

In this stillness, we find our light,
Guided by flames through the chilly night.
Together we weave this tender scene,
By candlelight, we reign supreme.

Sheltered Moments Amidst Chill

Within the room, the fire crackles,
Outside, the winter wind prattles.
Blankets piled in soft cascade,
A refuge from the cold parade.

Every heartbeat, a soft refrain,
Echoes sweet through windowpanes.
Laughter dances with the light,
As warm embraces chase the night.

In corners, shadows gently swell,
Whispering stories that time won't tell.
Each glance we share, a world of bliss,
In sheltered moments, we find our kiss.

The outside fades, our worries cease,
In this cocoon, we find our peace.
Though chill may linger, our hearts ignite,
In love's embrace, we hold each night.

Flickering Shadows on Icy Panes

As twilight falls, the shadows creep,
Woven tales in silence deep.
With every flicker, stories bloom,
In the warmth, we chase the gloom.

The icy breath on window glass,
Forms fleeting patterns as moments pass.
In playful dances, shadows blend,
A symphony where night won't end.

We gather close, the fire's glow,
Paints our faces with tales to show.
In every corner, memories shy,
Underneath the starlit sky.

Through frosty gold, our laughter spills,
With every heartbeat, joy fulfills.
Flickering lights in night's embrace,
Nurture love through winter's grace.

Hidden Sanctuaries of Light

In the shadowed depths they lie,
Soft whispers of the morning sky.
Each secret beam, a gentle touch,
In hidden nooks that mean so much.

The rustling leaves in sunlight dance,
As golden hues invite a glance.
Here, time unfolds with tender grace,
In tranquil spaces, we find our place.

Amidst the gloom, a spark will rise,
From hidden corners, dreams will guise.
A sanctuary, pure and bright,
Where weary souls reclaim their light.

Within each heart, a treasure's kept,
A garden where the spirit leapt.
Hidden sanctuaries await,
To guide the lost and celebrate.

The Solace of Stillness

In quiet moments, peace descends,
Where time halts, and sorrow mends.
The world outside fades into grey,
Yet inside, calmness finds its way.

A breath, a pause, the heart will sing,
In stillness, bloom the joys we bring.
The gentle hum of thoughts aligned,
In silent spaces, solace find.

The weight of days drifts far away,
As whispers of the night will sway.
In shadows where we seek to rest,
Amidst the quiet, we are blessed.

Stillness wraps us in its arms,
A refuge safe from worldly harms.
In the silence, love's embrace,
Finds its home in tranquil grace.

Fables by the Fire

Underneath a blanket sky,
Fables weave and flames reply.
In flickering light, tales come alive,
As laughter dances, hearts arrive.

Charmed by stories, young and old,
Whispers of courage, dreams retold.
Each ember glows with wisdom's lore,
In shared moments, we explore.

Faces illuminated, eyes aglow,
Each narrative a cherished flow.
With every tale, the night expands,
As time slips through our eager hands.

The bond of voices, warm and clear,
In every story, love draws near.
By firelight, our spirits soar,
Fables shared forevermore.

Flickers of Hope in the Frost

When winter's breath creates a chill,
And silent echoes seem to thrill,
Look close to see those tiny lights,
Flickers of hope in coldest nights.

Amidst the frost, new dreams arise,
Each glimmer sparks beneath grey skies.
In every flake, a promise holds,
A tale of warmth that still unfolds.

Though shadows stretch, the heart will fight,
To find the courage wrapped in light.
For every chill, a warmth will bloom,
With hope that chases away the gloom.

So gather strength in frozen breath,
Embrace the light that conquers death.
Flickers of hope will lead the way,
To brighter dawns and warmer days.

The Velvet of a Quiet Evening

The dusk drapes soft, a gentle sigh,
Whispers of night, as stars wink high.
Shadows dance in the cool, crisp air,
A tapestry woven with tender care.

Beneath the boughs where silence weaves,
Crickets serenade the falling leaves.
The world slows down, a peaceful retreat,
In the velvet moments where stillness meets.

Sipping Solitude by Candlelight

A flicker of flame casts shadows long,
In the quiet room, there's a soft song.
With each sip warms, sweet, secret delight,
Sipping solitude by the candlelight.

Pages turn in a gentle embrace,
Lost in the words, time slows down its race.
Embracing the silence, soft and profound,
In this sacred stillness, peace is found.

Gathering Clouds of Woolen Thoughts

Thoughts drift like clouds in a slow parade,
Woolen and warm, in the afternoon shade.
Ideas swirl, soft like the fluffs above,
Spun from the fabric of dreams and love.

Time folds gently, a comforting quilt,
Within this cocoon, no room for guilt.
Each moment lingers, a mindful embrace,
In the gathering clouds, I find my space.

Cradled in the Hush of Winter

Beneath the blanket of white calm lies,
The world in slumber, 'neath muted skies.
Frosted breath paints the branches bare,
Cradled in the hush, we breathe the air.

Snowflakes dance in the soft, still night,
Stars twinkle gently, a diamond sight.
In the heart of winter, warmth ignites,
Cradled in silence, the spirit takes flight.

Rustic Charm Beneath a Furry Throw

In a cabin kissed by dusk,
The fire crackles soft and low,
Wooden beams hold stories fresh,
Beneath a furry throw, we glow.

Candles dance with shadows' play,
The scent of pine fills the air,
Laughter lingers, gone astray,
Rustic charm, a cozy lair.

Outside the stars begin to peek,
While whispers weave around the room,
In this haven, silence speaks,
Wrapped in warmth, all fears consume.

Together here, our hearts entwine,
In moments treasured, time stands still,
Underneath this blanket fine,
Love's embrace, our spirits thrill.

Threading Memories in the Silence.

In gentle hush, the past awakes,
A tapestry of soft refrains,
Each thread a sigh, the heart now aches,
Memories danced in quiet lanes.

With every stitch, a story told,
In faded fabric, voices sing,
Whispers of youth, both brave and bold,
Time's gentle weavings ever cling.

Beneath the surface, dreams reside,
Like hidden treasures, softly sewn,
In silence deep, our hearts collide,
Threading the stories we have known.

In the stillness, echoes bloom,
A garden rich with hues of grace,
Casting light upon the gloom,
Threading memories, time we embrace.

Whispers of Warmth

A kindled flame in nightly gloom,
Cradles secrets, soft and bright,
Whispers of warmth within the room,
Enfolding all in gentle light.

Cups of cocoa, laughter shared,
Moments woven, sweet and near,
In every glance, our hearts declared,
The simple joys that bring us cheer.

Outside, the world grows cold and grey,
But in this space, the chill takes flight,
Wrapped in comfort, come what may,
The whispers keep the dark at bay.

Together in this quiet glow,
With tender hearts, we find our way,
In bonds of love, as rivers flow,
Whispers of warmth, our souls do sway.

Frosted Glass Murmurs

Through frosted glass, the world appears,
A dreamlike stillness hides the night,
Silent whispers melt our fears,
As snowflakes twirl in soft, pure light.

Each pane adorned with crystal lace,
Nature's art in silent grace,
Murmurs swirl in winter's embrace,
A ballet of shadows they trace.

In this wonderland, hearts entwine,
As frost-kissed breath paints fleeting sighs,
Moments frozen, pure and divine,
Gazing through with starry eyes.

With every glance, a secret kept,
Frosted glass holds stories rare,
In whispered dreams, our souls have leapt,
Carried softly on the air.

Hearthside Dreams

Whispers of warmth in the glow,
Soft blankets drape like a slow flow,
Embers dance in the quiet night,
While snowflakes twirl in the soft light.

Thoughts drift to places untold,
Where stories of yore gently unfold,
The heart finds peace in the soft hum,
As dreams echo where winter winds come.

The flicker of flames paints the air,
Painted tales only the night can share,
In this sacred space, we gather near,
Finding solace in moments sincere.

Warmth wraps us like a soft caress,
In heartbeats of silence, we feel blessed,
Here by the hearth, our spirits soar,
In the dance of shadows, we yearn for more.

Chilly Shadows and Flickering Flames

Chilly shadows creep on the wall,
The night whispers secrets, a soft call,
Flickering flames with a gentle sigh,
In the hearth's embrace, we learn to fly.

A circle of friends, laughter alight,
Together we banish the creeping fright,
Each crackle and pop tells a story true,
Of winter's hold and friendship anew.

Mugs of hot cocoa, steam rising high,
In this golden glow, time seems to fly,
The world outside, a frozen dream,
Within these walls, a warm, bright beam.

When the darkness deepens, we'll hold tight,
Finding comfort in the flickering light,
For every shadow that flickers and fades,
The hearth keeps us whole, in warmth cascades.

Snug Corners on Winter Nights

In snug corners where warmth resides,
We gather close, where love abides,
A blanket fort, a refuge sweet,
Where laughter dances, and hearts meet.

The wind howls outside, a chilling tune,
But inside's a glow like the bright moon,
Stories linger in the mellow air,
Crafted with care, a world we share.

Footsteps fade on the frosty ground,
In our cozy haven, peace is found,
Each flickering candle, a tiny spark,
Guiding us through the enveloping dark.

With every heartbeat, the moments sway,
In snug corners, we find our way,
Winter nights may be cold and long,
But here in our hearts, we always belong.

Embrace of the Winter Hearth

The embrace of the hearth, warm and alive,
A refuge of quiet where dreams thrive,
Crackling logs sing a melodic tune,
As shadows dance beneath the moon.

Woolen socks and whispers low,
Fireside tales mixed with gentle glow,
Outside the world wears a blanket of white,
Within, we find warmth and pure delight.

Pine-scented air, a comforting find,
As stories entwine, the future and mind,
Embers spark joy, flickers of past,
In the glow of the hearth, friendships are cast.

So come gather close, let your worries be light,
For this winter's embrace shines ever so bright,
In the flicker of flames, our hearts intertwine,
In the glow of the hearth, love forever shines.

Muffled Laughter Over Cold Breezes

In the park where shadows play,
Children's voices drift away.
Muffled laughter fills the air,
Colder winds catch moments rare.

Leaves rustle softly on the ground,
With every giggle, joy is found.
Echoes dance through frosty nights,
Heartstrings pulling, warm delights.

Branches sway, the moonlight glows,
Drawing us in where warmth bestows.
Every chuckle, every sigh,
Paints a memory passing by.

Breezes chill but spirits soar,
In laughter's spell, we yearn for more.
Together we weave a tale divine,
Muffled laughter, endless shrine.

The Overstuffed Chair's Embrace

In the corner where dreams reside,
An overstuffed chair, arms open wide.
It whispers tales of days gone by,
In its cushions, secrets lie.

With each slump into its grace,
Worries fade, time finds its pace.
Warmth envelops, a gentle hug,
As the world outside pulls and tugs.

Forgotten books and faded seams,
Hold echoes of all our dreams.
One more moment, just one more,
In this chair, worries are ignored.

Soft and worn, its fabric stained,
Yet within it, laughter is retained.
Embraced by memories, we unwind,
In that chair, solace we find.

Fragments of Warmth in the Air

Morning sun peeks through the haze,
Casting warmth in gentle rays.
Coffee brews, its scent a song,
In this moment, we belong.

Birds chirp softly, a sweet refrain,
As dreams weave through the windowpane.
Fragments of warmth dance and play,
Chasing the chill of a fading day.

Laughter rises, echoing bright,
Finding comfort in shared light.
Connections spark, like fires ignite,
Turning whispers into flight.

In every breath, the world feels near,
Fragments of warmth that draw us here.
Countless moments woven tight,
In the quiet, hearts unite.

An Evening Wrapped in Thorns

Twilight drapes its velvet shroud,
While shadows gather, dark and proud.
Thorns entwined in every space,
Holding secrets, soft embrace.

Whispers mix with fragrant night,
As stars emerge with soft delight.
Each thorn tells tales of love and pain,
In nature's heart, what's lost remains.

Amidst the beauty, hardness lies,
An evening touched by darkened skies.
Yet hope endures, despite the fray,
Finding light within the gray.

Wrapped in thorns, the night unfolds,
Tales of courage, softly told.
So as we wander, hand in hand,
We embrace the thorns, understand.

Harvest of Comfort from the Winter's Bounty

Golden fields now bare and cold,
Yet hearts aglow with warmth untold.
Gathering memories like the grain,
A gentle touch through winter's pain.

Frosty breath and starlit skies,
Laughter echoes, soft replies.
In the harvest, find your peace,
Let the winter's chill release.

Cozy corners, candles light,
Stories shared deep into night.
Count the blessings small and bright,
Hold them close, through the longest night.

When spring arrives, new blooms in sight,
We'll cherish warmth, our hearts take flight.
Bounty gathered, love's embrace,
In winter's grip, we find our place.

Through the Lattice: A View of Warmth

Through the lattice, sunbeams creep,
Warming hearts coaxed from sleep.
Each shadow dances, light entwined,
In this window, solace find.

Winter's chill may steal the day,
Yet through the glass, the light will play.
Hope ignites in golden threads,
As whispers weave from sleepy beds.

Crimson leaves in gentle sway,
A tapestry of yesterday.
Through the panes, a world unfolds,
Stories stitched with warmth, so bold.

Let the breeze that enters here,
Carry laughter, chase the fear.
Through the lattice, love shines bright,
In the darkness, we find light.

Secrets Kept Behind Glass Panes

Behind the glass, stories reside,
Silent whispers, dreams abide.
Frosted edges, thoughts concealed,
In these panes, our hearts revealed.

Ghostly figures dance and sway,
Moments cherished, kept at bay.
Hushed confessions, softly spoken,
In the quiet, bonds unbroken.

Snowflakes falling, secrets drift,
In the stillness, kindness lift.
Within these walls, a world unsealed,
Every glance, a fate revealed.

As the night draws shadows near,
We find comfort, hold it dear.
In the glass where stories blend,
Love remains, it will not end.

The Stillness Between the Drifts

In the stillness, whispers sigh,
Gentle breezes flutter by.
Between the drifts, a quiet peace,
Moments linger, never cease.

Softly falling, snow and night,
Blanket over, purest white.
In silence held, a time to dream,
Thoughts like rivers, softly stream.

Traces left on barren ground,
Each heartbeat, a soothing sound.
Winter's breath speaks secrets low,
In the stillness, love will grow.

Here, in the quietude we stay,
Finding warmth in nature's sway.
As seasons fade, we'll hold this place,
In the stillness, find our grace.

Constellations of Comfort in the Air

Whispers of night softly call,
Stars twinkle bright, a blanket for all.
In the hush, dreams take flight,
Comfort of constellations, a guiding light.

Breezes carry secrets untold,
Stories of warmth wrapped in gold.
Each twinkle, a promise to share,
Constellations of comfort, floating in air.

Night's embrace tender and deep,
In cosmic arms, we safely sleep.
Dreams woven with stardust so fair,
Under the watch of the heavens' care.

Embers of night flicker and gleam,
In the dark, we find our dream.
Among the stars, we find our way,
Comforted by constellations each day.

Twilight Tucked in Between Soft Throws

Twilight whispers, a gentle sigh,
Golden hues bleed into the sky.
Soft throws drape over dreams anew,
Nestled in warmth, the world feels true.

Shadows dance in the fading light,
Cocooned in comfort, we hold on tight.
Each moment wrapped in twilight's glow,
In this stillness, our hearts will grow.

Silken threads weave tales of night,
Where laughter mingles, taking flight.
Between soft throws, all worries cease,
Wrapped in twilight, we find our peace.

As stars peek through the dusk's embrace,
Every heartbeat slows, a sacred space.
In the glow of evening's tender glow,
Twilight's magic cradles us slow.

Gentle Morning Under Frosty Veils

Morning whispers through frosty panes,
A gentle light melts winter's chains.
Each breath a cloud in the crisp air,
Under veils of frost, waking with care.

Soft sunlight kisses the ground,
In this hush, such beauty is found.
Frosty patterns glimmer and shine,
Morning's magic, a gift divine.

Nature awakens, pearls of dew,
A tranquil silence where dreams renew.
In the glow of a day so clear,
Gentle morning, we hold you dear.

Wrapped in warmth, we greet the day,
With every breath, worries drift away.
Under frosty veils, life's sweet embrace,
Morning's promise, a gentle grace.

Wrapped in Silken Dreams

Silken threads weave a soft retreat,
Where dreams entwine, our hearts will meet.
In gentle whispers, the night unfolds,
Wrapped in dreams, our story told.

Moonlight dances on shadows cast,
In this realm, time slips away fast.
Each sigh a secret, tender and deep,
Wrapped in silken dreams, peacefully sleep.

Fantasy flows like a river wide,
With every heartbeat, we take a ride.
In this cocoon, all worries cease,
Wrapped in dreams, we find our peace.

Stars become stories, each twinkling a spark,
Illuminating paths through the dark.
In the hush of night, love's soft beams,
We drift together, wrapped in dreams.

The Embrace of a Woven Hearth

In the glow of dusk, we gather near,
Woven tales and laughter fill the air.
Hearts entwined like threads in cloth,
A warmth that wraps us, soft and froth.

The fire crackles, stories unfold,
In every ember, memories told.
Hands reach out for the felted embrace,
In this cozy haven, we find our place.

With every sip of spiced cider warm,
We cast away doubt, find shelter from storm.
The woven hearth holds dreams and cheer,
A tender refuge, drawing us near.

As shadows dance and daylight fades,
The essence of home in every shade.
Each moment cherished, time stands still,
In the woven hearth, we find our will.

Snowflakes on the Inside

Outside the window, snowflakes fall,
But inside blooms, a warm soft call.
A blanket wrapped, we settle tight,
With the world outside, a shimmering sight.

Each flake a whisper, pure and bright,
Stories of winter, a magical light.
Yet, in here, the chill can't intrude,
Our hearts resound in a cozy mood.

With cocoa brewed, we clink our mugs,
In every sip, are warm, sweet hugs.
Snowflakes dance, but we stand still,
In comfort's lap, against the chill.

As time meanders through the night,
Inside our fortress, everything is right.
Each snowflake falling just outside,
While warmth envelops, we coincide.

Heartfelt Huddles in Hidden Corners

In corners hidden, where shadows twine,
We huddle close, your hand in mine.
Soft whispers shared, secrets unfold,
In the warmth of hearts, our stories told.

The world outside may rise and fall,
But here in safety, we share it all.
An ember glows, a gentle fire,
Wrapped in love, we soar higher.

With laughter ringing, the night feels bright,
In our cozy nook, we find our light.
Each moment cherished, time held fast,
In heartfelt huddles, we build our past.

When storms may shake, and fears take flight,
We draw together, two souls ignite.
In hidden corners, we know the art,
A bond unbreakable, heart to heart.

Chill Outside, Glow Within

The wind may howl, the frost may bite,
Yet here we dwell, in the warm twilight.
The chill outside, a distant song,
In the hearth's embrace, we belong.

With laughter shared, we chase away gloom,
Our spirits dance, lighting the room.
The world may shiver, but here we thrive,
In our glow within, we feel alive.

Snowflakes gather on the windowpane,
While inside, love flows like gentle rain.
A flickering flame, a whispered vow,
In our haven here, we make it now.

So let the winter's harshness be,
For in our hearts, there's symmetry.
Chill outside can never sway,
The warmth we share, come what may.

The Warmth of Togetherness

In the glow of laughter bright,
Hands entwined, we feel the light.
Moments shared, hearts open wide,
In this warmth, we never hide.

With every smile, a bond is formed,
Through storms and trials, we are warmed.
Close as shadows in the night,
Together we make the world feel right.

In silence or in joyous song,
Where we belong, we will be strong.
The warmth of love, sweet and pure,
In this togetherness, we endure.

Through every season, hand in hand,
In unity, we make our stand.
The warmth of togetherness we seek,
In every word, in every peak.

Crystal Veils and Gentle Flames

Underneath the starry skies,
Dance the dreams with whispered sighs.
Crystal veils that softly gleam,
Dancing flames in twilight's dream.

Colors fuse in evening's embrace,
Reflecting life, a sacred space.
Glimmers of hope in every glance,
We find our peace in this gentle dance.

Echoes of laughter linger here,
As love's sweet music fills the sphere.
With every spark, a story told,
In crystal veils, our hearts unfold.

Through tender moments, soft and bright,
We chase the shadows, bring the light.
Gentle flames that warm the air,
In their glow, we find our care.

Enchanted Evening Retreats

In twilight's hush, we steal away,
To secret spots where dreamers play.
Enchanted moments, softly shared,
In every glance, we are prepared.

Beneath the leaves, where whispers croon,
The stars will guide us to our tune.
A serenade that fills the night,
In perfect union, hearts take flight.

With every step, the world holds breath,
In quiet wonder, we find depth.
Retreats of magic, time stands still,
Together weaving dreams at will.

In soft-lit paths, we lose the day,
With every moment, come what may.
These evenings crafted, pure and sweet,
Are cherished tales where lovers meet.

Heartfelt Conversations by the Hearth

By the hearth, the fire glows,
Bringing warmth as soft wind blows.
Heartfelt chats that weave our tales,
In this space, love never fails.

With every story, laughter rings,
Shared hopes and dreams take gentle wings.
Wisdom blooms where hearts align,
In this shelter, we define.

The crackling flames, our timeless muse,
Inviting thoughts we won't refuse.
In every pause, connections grow,
As shadows dance in flickered glow.

Together, we will brave the night,
Heartfelt bonds, forever bright.
By the hearth, our souls convene,
In every word, we weave the dream.

Tender Hues of Comfort

In twilight's soft embrace we find,
A touch of warmth to ease the mind.
With gentle whispers, colors blend,
A canvas where our hearts can mend.

Like petals drifting on the breeze,
Each moment cradles us with ease.
In shades of peach and lavender,
We weave the threads of love's defer.

The sunset blush, a sweet refrain,
In tender hues, we shed our pain.
As twilight deepens, stars appear,
In comfort's arms, we hold what's dear.

Each color speaks of memories,
Of laughter shared beneath the trees.
In evening's glow, our spirits soar,
In tender hues, forevermore.

Silent Snowfall and Gentle Glow

In whispers of the falling snow,
A tranquil peace begins to flow.
The world adorns its frosty dress,
In silence wrapped, we feel the bless.

The moonlight casts a silver sheen,
On sheets of white, so pure, serene.
Each flake, a story, soft, unique,
In gentle glow, our hearts can speak.

Beneath the stars, we wander slow,
Through winter's charm, a gentle show.
In frosty air, our laughter plays,
As time dissolves in snowy maze.

A hug of warmth, a hand to hold,
Through silent nights, our dreams unfold.
In every flake, a whispered wish,
A dance of peace, a timeless bliss.

Warmth Beneath Woolen Throws

Wrapped in layers soft and tight,
We nestle close on winter nights.
The crackling fire, a glowing heart,
In woolen throws, we won't depart.

With every stitch, a tale is spun,
A haven found, two souls as one.
Embraced by warmth, the world fades away,
In cozy corners where we play.

The chilly winds may howl outside,
But here, within, our dreams abide.
With laughter shared and love aglow,
In warmth we find, a gentle flow.

As embers fade and eyelids close,
In tranquil air, the stillness grows.
Together wrapped in bedtime's grace,
In woolen throws, our sacred space.

Radiance in the Frost

In frosted fields where silence reigns,
A world of white, no trace of chains.
Each branch adorned with crystal lace,
In winter's grip, we find our place.

The sun breaks through with golden beams,
Awakening the land from dreams.
A radiance that warms the chill,
In tranquil moments, hearts can fill.

Each breath a cloud, a fleeting thought,
In depths of winter, solace wrought.
As light reflects on icy ground,
In nature's arms, our peace is found.

With every step, the crisp air sings,
Of fleeting joy that winter brings.
In radiance bright, our spirits glide,
In frost's embrace, we shall reside.

Frost-Covered Corners and Evocative Silence

In corners cold, where shadows play,
Frost lies thick, the light in gray.
A breath of winter, sharp and clear,
Silence reigns, the world austere.

Each crystal glints on branches bare,
Whispers of secrets in the air.
Memories drift on icy breath,
Softly dancing, welcoming death.

Twilight bends as dusk descends,
Nature sleeps, and time suspends.
Frost-covered dreams in shades of white,
Echoes linger through the night.

In this stillness, hearts may find,
What solitude has left behind.
Embrace the chill, the quiet grace,
In frost-covered corners, find your place.

Tucked Away in Timelessness

In a wooden chest, dreams conceal,
Tucked away, the past feels real.
Photographs and letters worn,
Whispers of love, the heart reborn.

Pages yellowed with age and time,
Stories echo in silent rhyme.
A locket's glow, a soft caress,
In timelessness, there's no duress.

Hours drift like petals in flight,
Moments held beneath starlight.
Memory's quilt, stitched with care,
Wraps the soul in warmth, a prayer.

Tucked away from the world outside,
In stillness, dreams and hopes abide.
With every glance, the heart can see,
Life's simple joys, a tapestry.

The Stillness Wrapped in a Soft Embrace

In morning light, the world awakes,
Stillness wraps like gentle flakes.
Whispers stroke the quiet morn,
Soft embrace where peace is born.

The trees stand tall, their branches sway,
Nature's hymn in grand display.
Birds on branches sing their tune,
A serenade 'neath the golden moon.

Clouds drift lazily in the blue,
Moments linger, fresh and new.
In golden rays, shadows blend,
Time slows down, a perfect mend.

Wrapped in softness, breath reveals,
The stillness where the heart appeals.
A tranquil wave, the day begins,
In quietude, the soul finds kin.

Wisps of Steam and Whispers of Home

In the kitchen, warmth unfolds,
Wisps of steam, stories told.
The kettle sings, a gentle sound,
Whispers of home forever found.

A spice of cinnamon fills the air,
Comfort lingers everywhere.
Family laughter, a cherished song,
In these moments, we belong.

The table set with love's embrace,
Every meal, a sacred space.
Hands entwined, grateful hearts,
In this dance, life's beauty starts.

As dusk descends and candles glow,
Memories formed, and love will grow.
In wisps of steam, the heart will roam,
Forever stitched, the fabric of home.

Shadows and Stillness at Twilight

Shadows weave 'neath fading light,
Whispers of the coming night.
Trees stand tall, their secrets kept,
In quiet realms where dreams are slept.

Stars awaken in the sky,
Glimmers where the wishes lie.
Softly now, the world holds breath,
As twilight dances close to death.

Ghostly echoes gently sway,
In the twilight's muted play.
Moments pause, the heart can feel,
The silent world begins to heal.

In the dusk, all worries fade,
Wrapped in peace, the night's cascade.
Shadows blend with the night's embrace,
A sanctuary, a tranquil space.

Kindling Comfort Against the Chill

Fires crackle in the gloom,
Casting warmth within the room.
Softly glows the amber light,
Chasing shadows of the night.

Blankets wrap like tender sighs,
In this warmth, no heart denies.
Cocoa steams in cups held tight,
Comfort found in each delight.

Memories drift in fragrant air,
Laughter lingers everywhere.
Togetherness, a rare embrace,
Kindling joy in winter's face.

Outside, the cold winds roar and bite,
But inside glows the fire bright.
Here, we weave our tales anew,
Against the chill, our spirits flew.

Hearth Bound Wishes

By the hearth, our wishes glow,
Softly spoken, not too slow.
Embers dancing, what a sight,
Guiding hopes into the night.

Each desire a flickering flame,
Binding hearts without a name.
Whispers echo through the years,
Crafted from our hopes and fears.

Together, we stoke the fire,
Tending dreams, growing higher.
In the warmth, our spirits soar,
Finding solace evermore.

As the twilight drapes its shroud,
In the silence, we feel proud.
Hearth bound wishes, bright and true,
Anchor us, as night renews.

A Symphony of Silence

In stillness, melodies reside,
A symphony where dreams abide.
Softest notes in shadows dance,
Embraced by calm, a fleeting glance.

The hush reveals the heart's deep song,
In silence, where we all belong.
Every breath, a gentle tune,
Chasing echoes of the moon.

Though the world outside may roar,
Within the stillness, we explore.
Nature's lullaby takes flight,
A whispered star against the night.

Here, in quiet, peace is found,
In solitude, our souls unbound.
A symphony, not loud, but clear,
In silence, we embrace what's dear.